ESSENTIAL EXERCISES AND ETUDES

for VIOLA

by HARVEY S. WHISTLER

T0057729

CONTENTS

HAL•LEONARD CORPORATION

7777 W. BLUEMOUND RD. P.O. BOX 13819 MILWAUKEE, WI 53213

Developing Bowing

WHISTLER

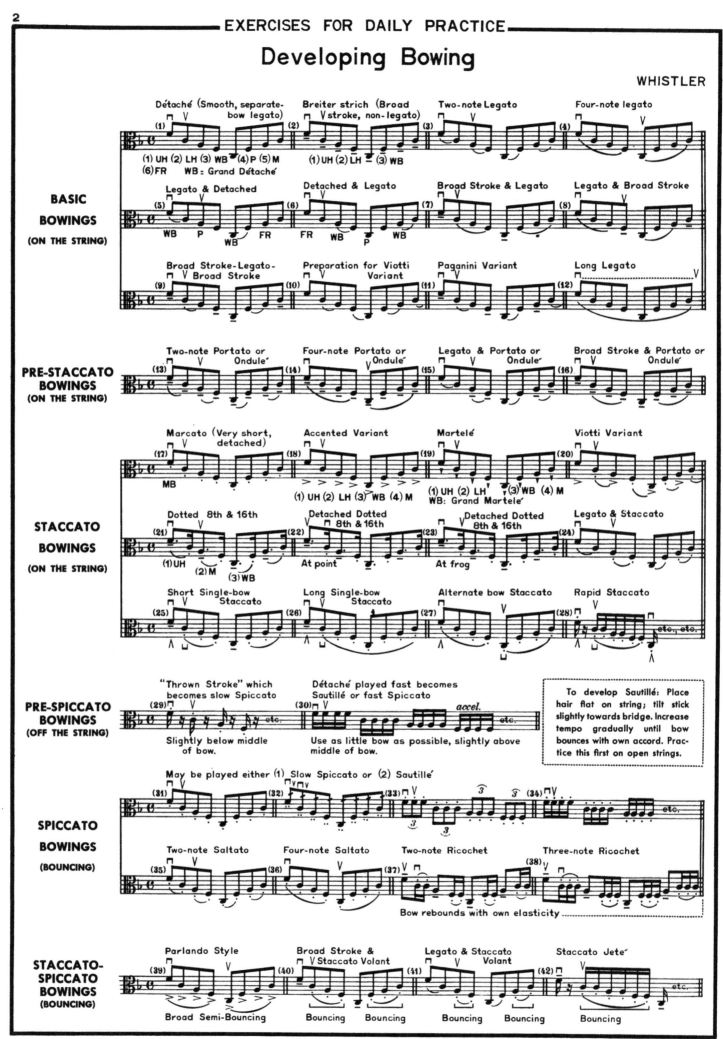

Etude for Developing Bowing

HOFMANN-WHISTLER

To be memorized. All bowing variants of opposite page should be systematically applied to this etude.

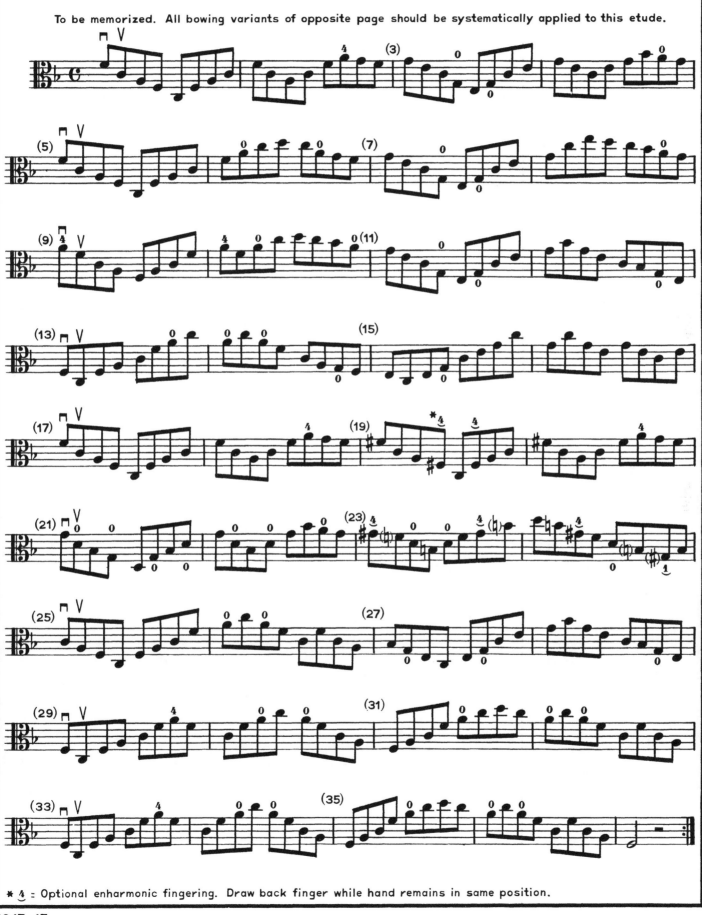

* 4 = Optional enharmonic fingering. Draw back finger while hand remains in same position.

Developing Digital Strength

WHISTLER

Practice slowly at first. Repeat each exercise many times.

◇ = Finger to be held down, but not active in producing a tone.

Developing Digital Independence

WHISTLER

Strike all fingers firmly, audibly, and with equal force on the string.

Play slowly at first, later increasing tempo.

Also practice lines IV through VII on the G, D and A strings.

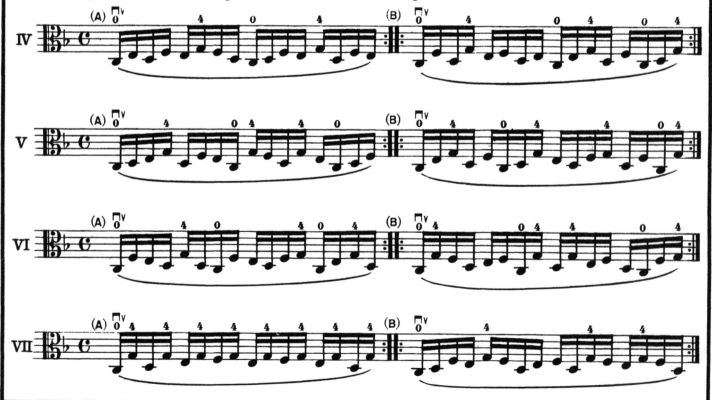

Etude in C

WEISS

To be played with broad strokes of the bow.

Also practice using (1) détaché bowings, as well as other basic variants, (2) selected staccato variants, and (3) selected spiccato variants.

Etude in F

WEISS

To be played in legato style.

Also practice using (1) détaché bowings, as well as other basic variants, (2) selected staccato variants, and (3) selected spiccato variants.

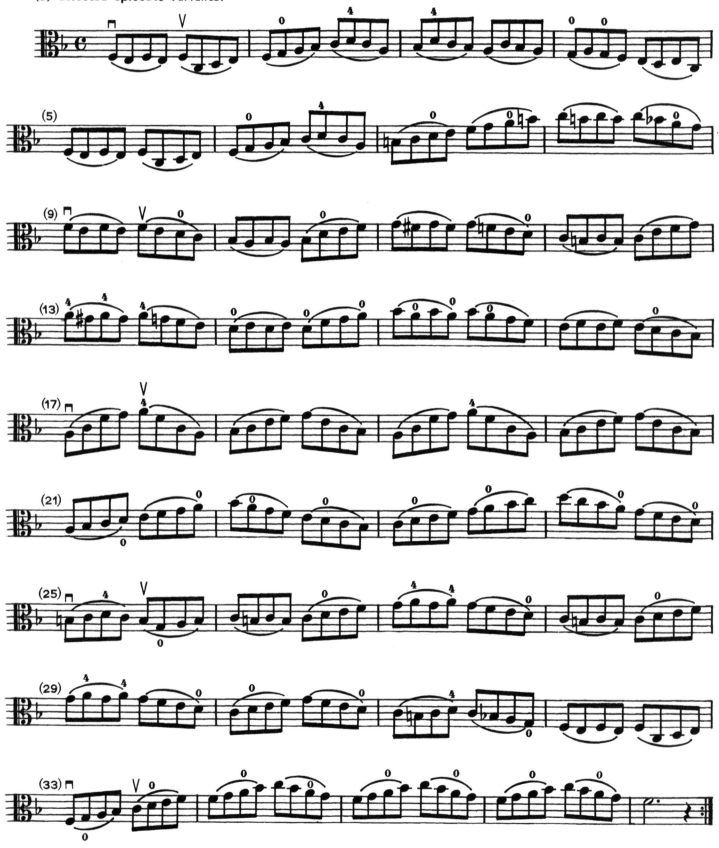

Etude in B♭

KAYSER

Maintain a firm, steady bow throughout. Observe proper bow division at all times.

Etude in G

HOFMANN

To be played in a firm, forceful manner. Maintain a steady tempo throughout.

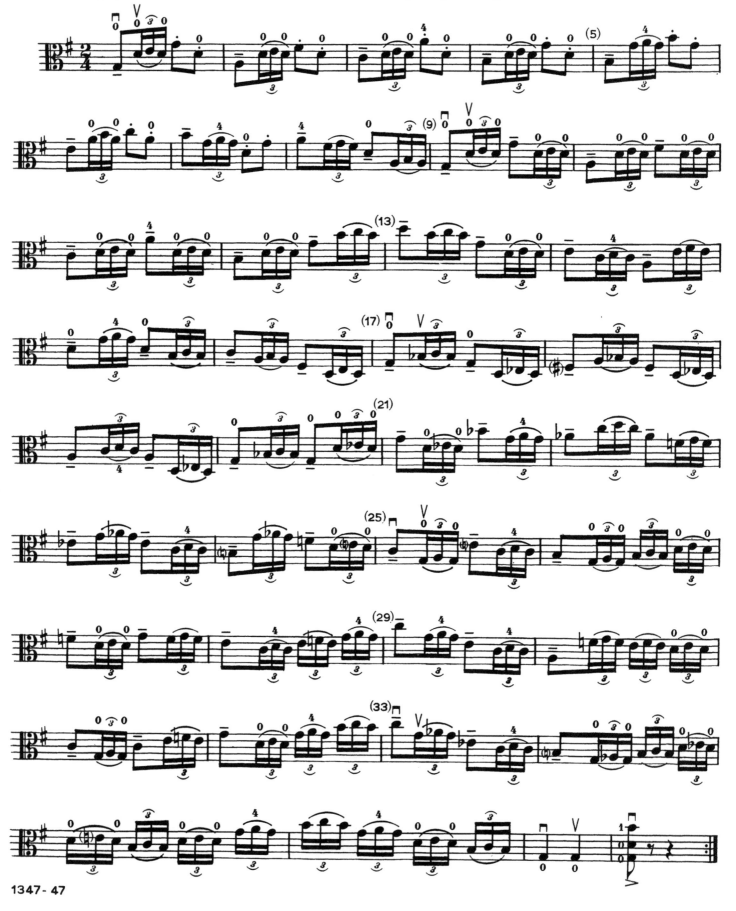

Etude in D

MAZAS

To be played in legato style. Maintain a smooth, steady tempo throughout.

Etude in E♭

SITT

To be played in legato style. Maintain a smooth, steady tempo throughout.

Etude in A♭

DE BERIOT

To be played in legato style.

Also practice slurring only four notes in each bow.

Also practice using (1) détaché bowings, as well as other basic variants, (2) selected staccato variants, and (3) selected spiccato variants.

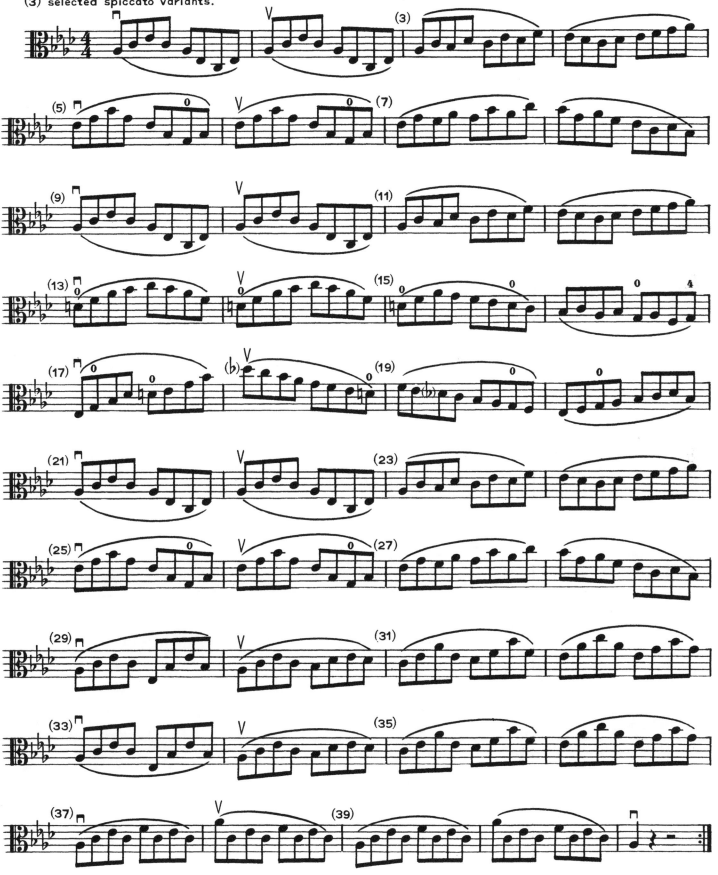

Etude in A

WOHLFAHRT

To be played with spiccato bowing, using selected variants of same.

Also practice using (1) détaché bowings, as well as other basic variants, and (2) selected staccato variants.

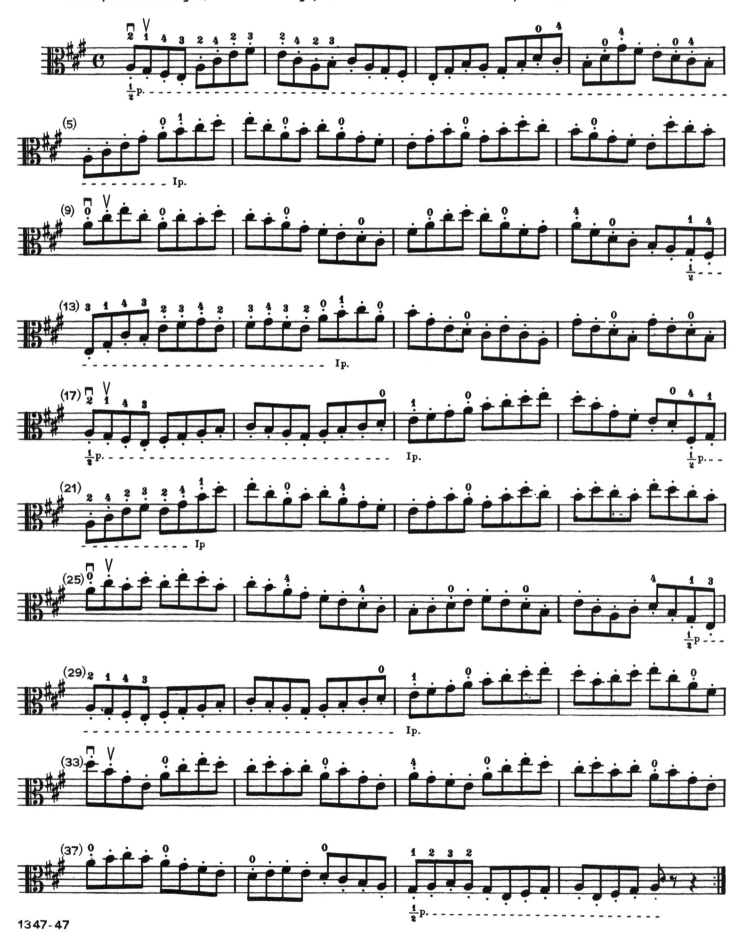

Etude in E

BÖHMER

Also practice using (1) détaché bowings, as well as other basic variants, (2) selected staccato variants, and (3) selected spiccato variants.

Legato Etude No. 1

SPOHR

To be played in legato style. Maintain a smooth, steady tempo throughout.
Also practice (1) with a separate bow for each tone, and (2) pizzicato.

Legato Etude No. 2

BÖHMER

To be played in legato style. Maintain a smooth, steady tempo throughout.

Also practice (1) with a separate bow for each tone, (2) slurring each four tones, (3) slurring each complete measure, and (4) pizzicato.

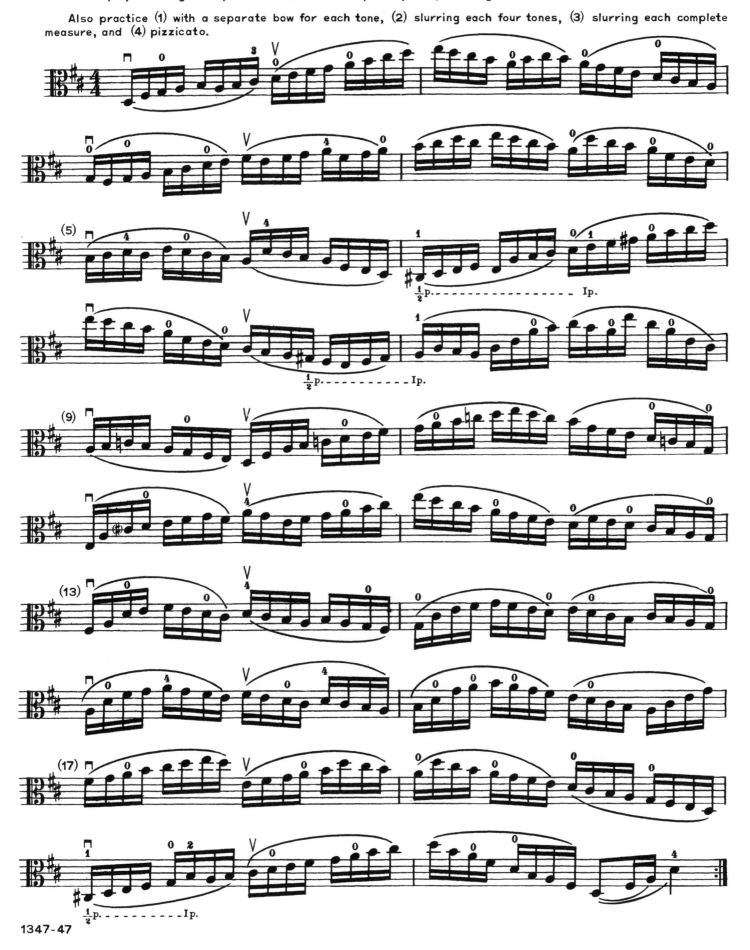

1347-47

Rhythmical Etude No.1

WOHLFAHRT

The dotted eighth note should be broad in effect, and the sixteenth note that follows, short and abrupt.

Rhythmical Etude No. 2

BÖHMER

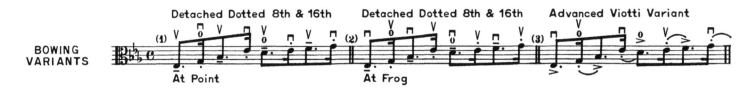

The dotted eighth note should be broad in effect, and the sixteenth note that follows, short and abrupt.

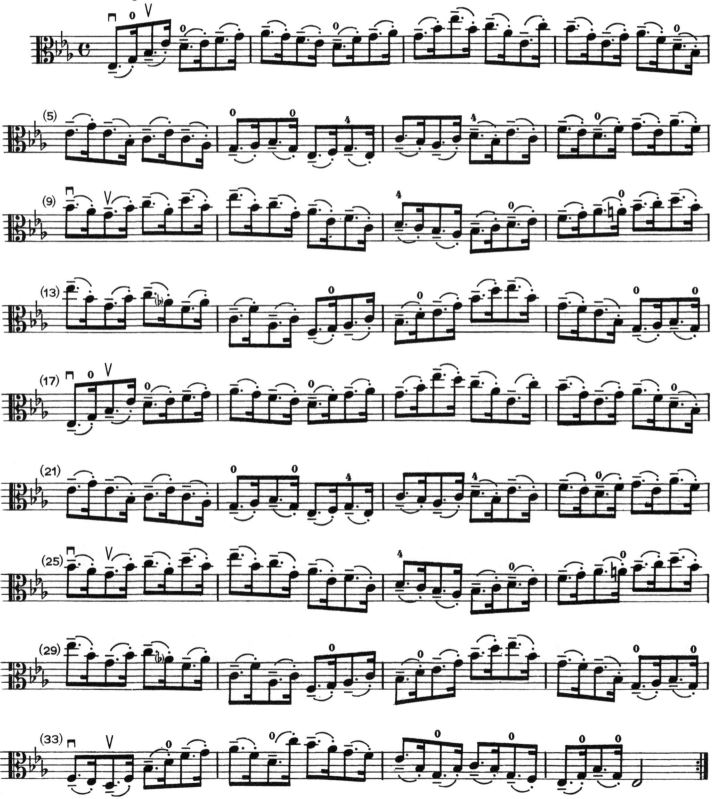

1347-47

Cross-Fingering Etude

ALARD

⌣ = Draw back finger while hand remains in same position.

Also practice (1) using a separate bow for each note, and (2) slurring each complete measure.

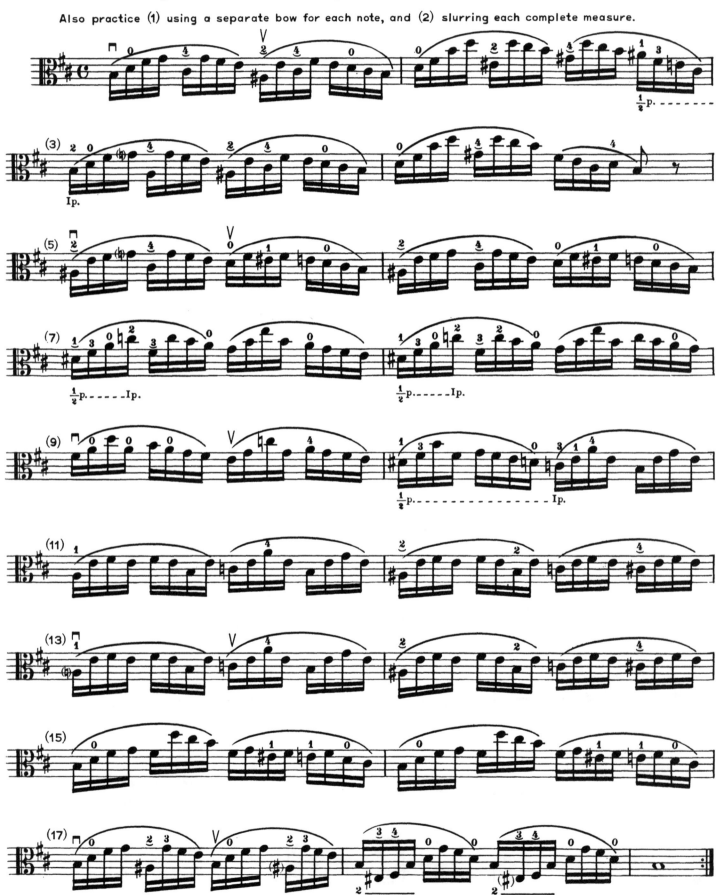

Spiccato Etude No. 1

KAYSER

To be played using (1) slow spiccato bowing and (2) sautillé bowing.

Also practice using other spiccato variants.

Spiccato Etude No. 2

CAMPAGNOLI

To be played using (1) slow spiccato bowing and (2) sautillé bowing.

Also practice using other spiccato variants.

Spiccato Etude No. 3

WOHLFAHRT

To be played with spiccato bowing, using selected variants of same.

Also practice using (1) détaché bowings, as well as other basic variants, and (2) selected staccato variants.

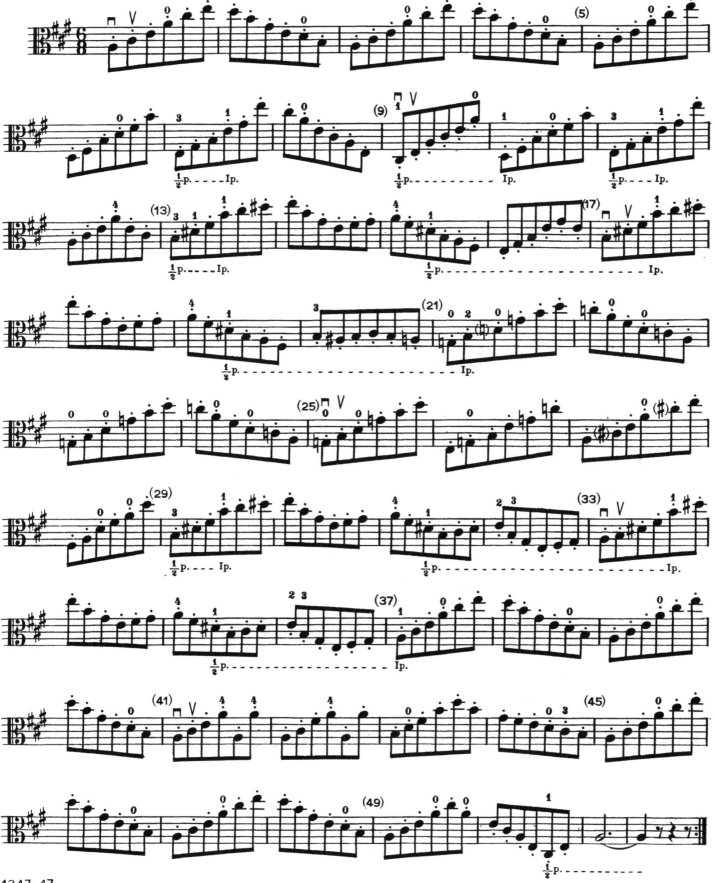

String-Crossing Etude No. 1

KAYSER

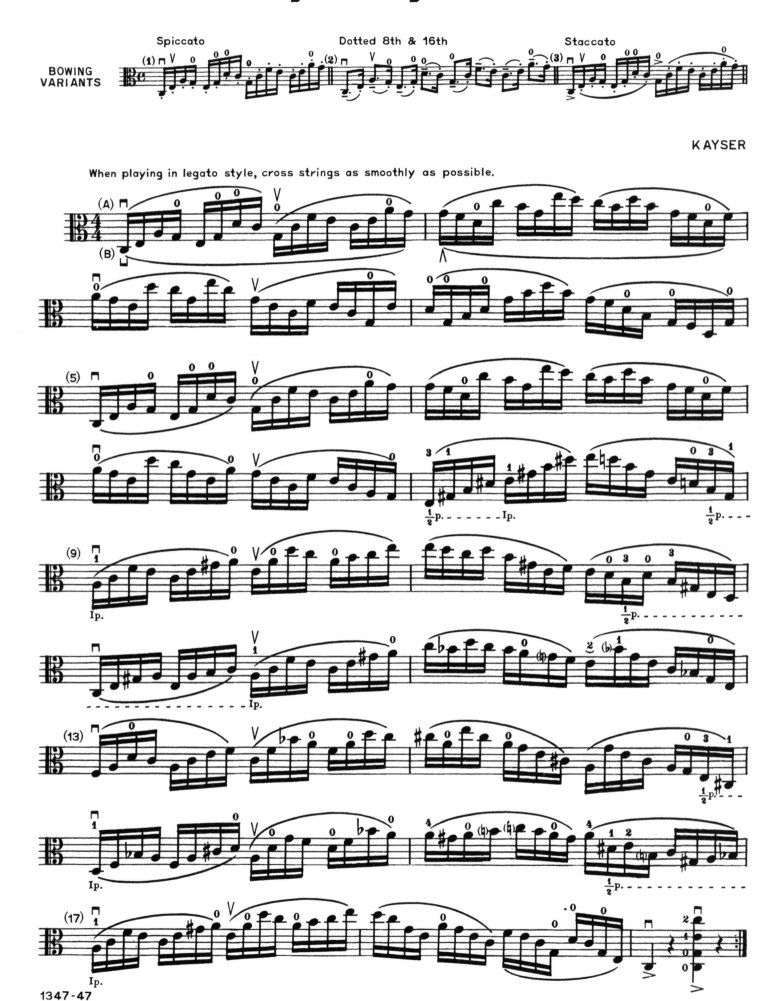

String-Crossing Etude No. 2

When playing in legato style, cross strings as smoothly as possible.

String-Skipping Etude

CAMPAGNOLI

To be played strictly in marcato style. Strings passed over should not be touched with the bow at the time of transfer.

Chromatic Etude

ASCENDING FINGER PATTERN	DESCENDING FINGER PATTERN
0-1-1-2-2-3-4	4-3-2-2-1-1-0

SITT

Practice slowly at first. Maintain a steady tempo throughout, Also practice using a separate bow for each note.

Advanced Chromatic Etude

ASCENDING FINGER PATTERN
0-1-1-2-2-3-4

DESCENDING FINGER PATTERN
4-3-2-2-1-1-0

SPOHR

Practice slowly at first. Maintain a steady tempo throughout.

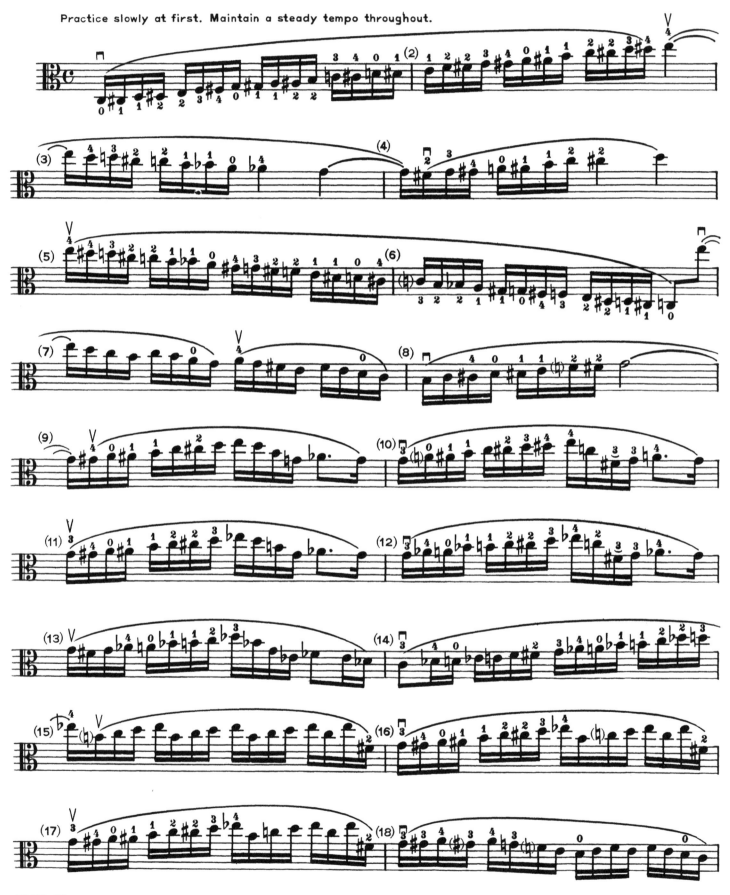

Arpeggio Etude

KAYSER

Keep fingers down as long as possible. All string transfers should be smooth throughout. Maintain a steady tempo at all times.

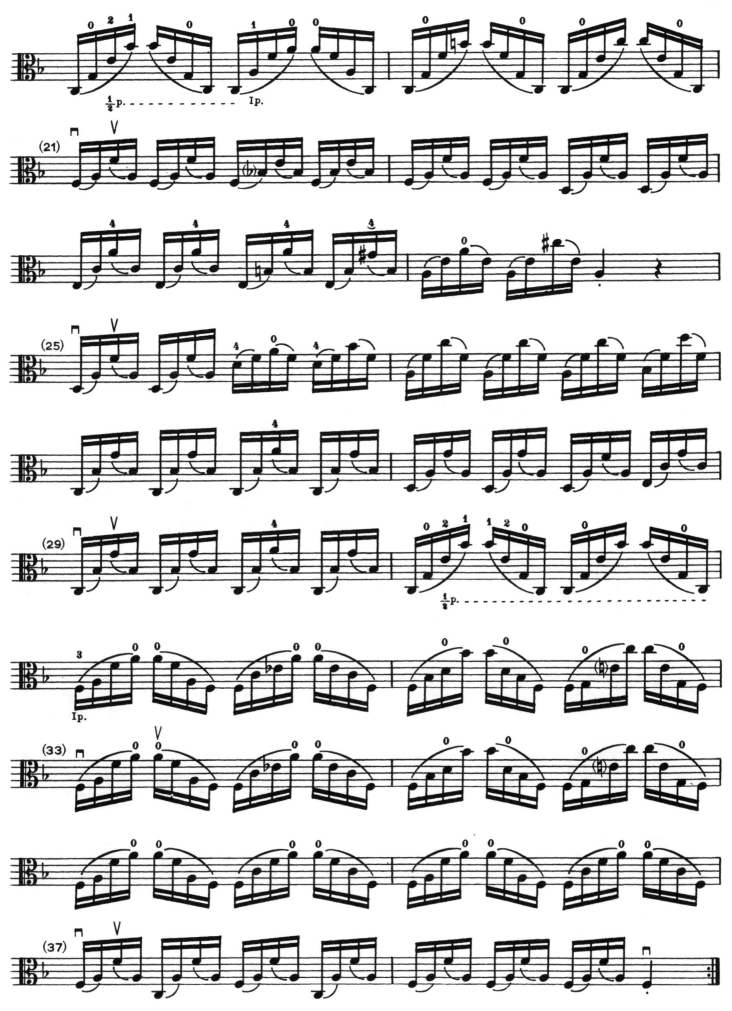

Syncopated Etude No. 1

ALARD

Practice slowly at first. If syncopated rhythmical problems arise, play individual measures as exercises, repeating them until the difficulties contained therein are mastered.

Syncopated Etude No. 2

WOHLFAHRT

Practice slowly at first. If syncopated rhythmical problems arise, play individual measures as exercises, repeating them until the difficulties contained therein are mastered.

Staccato Etude No. 1

WOHLFAHRT

Play the staccato notes in an abrupt, crisp manner. Each staccato tone should be clear, but short, and with individual emphasis on it.

Staccato Etude No. 2

DANCLA

Play the staccato notes in an abrupt, crisp manner. Each staccato tone should be clear, but short, and with individual emphasis on it.

Staccato Etude No. 3

DANCLA

Play the staccato notes in an abrupt, crisp manner. Each staccato tone should be clear, but short, and with individual emphasis on it.

Developing Trill Playing

WHISTLER

BASIC STUDIES

Practice similar exercises on the D, G, & C strings.

FOUNDATION STUDIES

Play each 32nd note with as much rapidity as possible, the trill finger rebounding with elasticity and speed. Gradually increase tempo until each exercise becomes a trill. It does not matter how many notes a trill contains; the greater the number of notes, the better the trill will sound. Repeat each line many times.

Practice similar exercises on the D, G, & C strings.

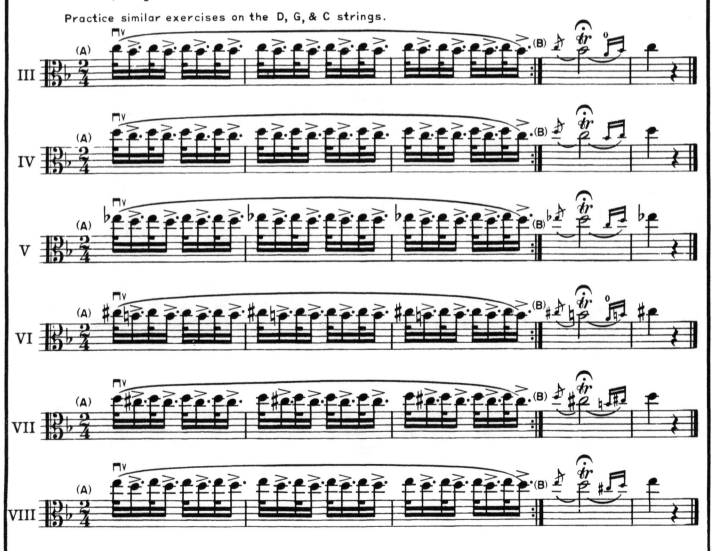

Trill Etude No. 1
(Half-Note Trills)

WOHLFAHRT

Play as many notes as possible in each trill; the greater the number of notes, the better the trill will sound.
Raise trill finger with rapid, light action.

Trill Etude No. 2
(Quarter-Note Trills)

WEISS

Play as many notes as possible in each trill. Raise trill finger with rapid, light action.

Also practice each trill starting with the principal note, disregarding the acciaccatura.

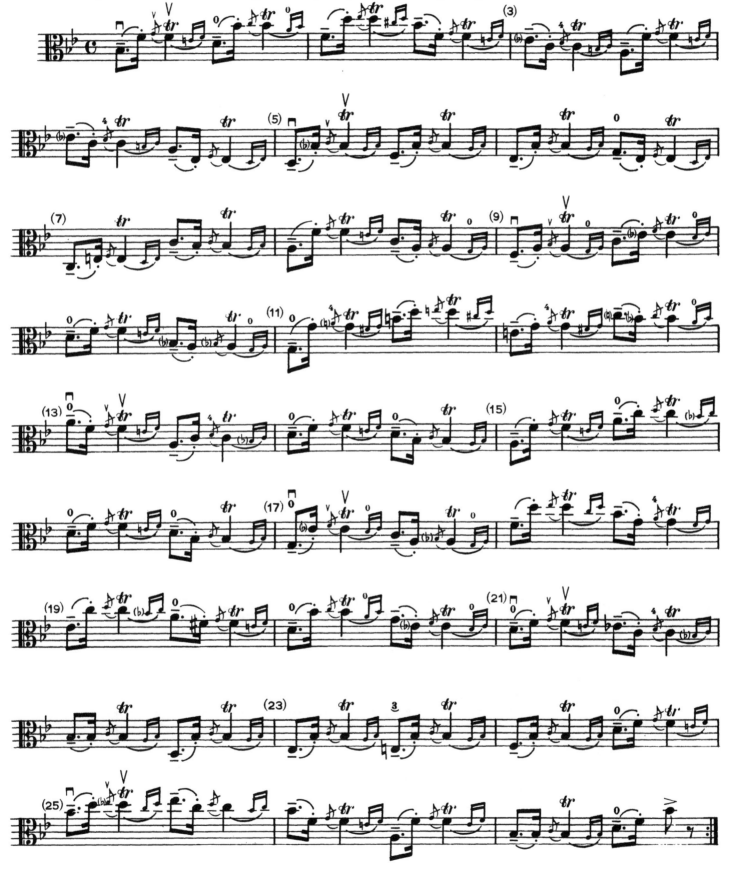

Developing Double-Stops

DE BERIOT

When playing double-stops, equal finger and bow pressures should be used at all times.

Practice slowly. Do not proceed from one interval to the next until the intonation is correct.

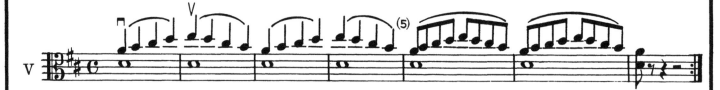

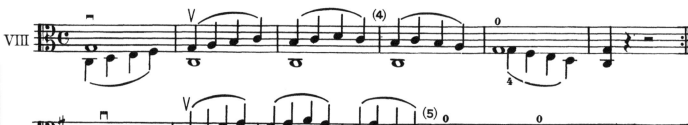

Double-Stop Etude No. 1 in F

SITT

To be played in legato style. Care should be taken to see that equal finger and bow pressures are used when producing each tone of the intervals.

Double-Stop Etude No. 2 in F

SITT

To be played in legato style. Care should be taken to see that equal finger and bow pressures are used when producing each tone of the intervals.

Double-Stop Etude in B♭

SITT

Maintain a steady tempo throughout. Do not proceed from any chord or double-stop to the next note or double-stop until the intonation is correct.

Double-Stop Etude in C

SITT

To be played in legato style. Care should be taken to see that equal finger and bow pressures are used when producing each tone of the intervals.

Double-Stop Etude in G

SITT

To be played in legato style. Care should be taken to see that equal finger and bow pressures are used when producing each tone of the intervals.

Double-Stop Etude in D

SITT

Also practice using a separate bow for each interval. Care should be taken to see that equal finger and bow pressures are used when producing each tone of the intervals.

Chordal Etude

DE BERIOT

In order to test intonation first play the lower and middle tones together, immediately tilting the bow and playing the middle and upper tones together. Gradually the tones of the three-note chords should be played simultaneously.

Etude de Concertante

L. SCHUBERT

Practice slowly at first. Maintain a steady tempo throughout. If rhythmical or technical problems arise, play individual measures as exercises, repeating them until the difficulties contained therein are reduced to a minimum.

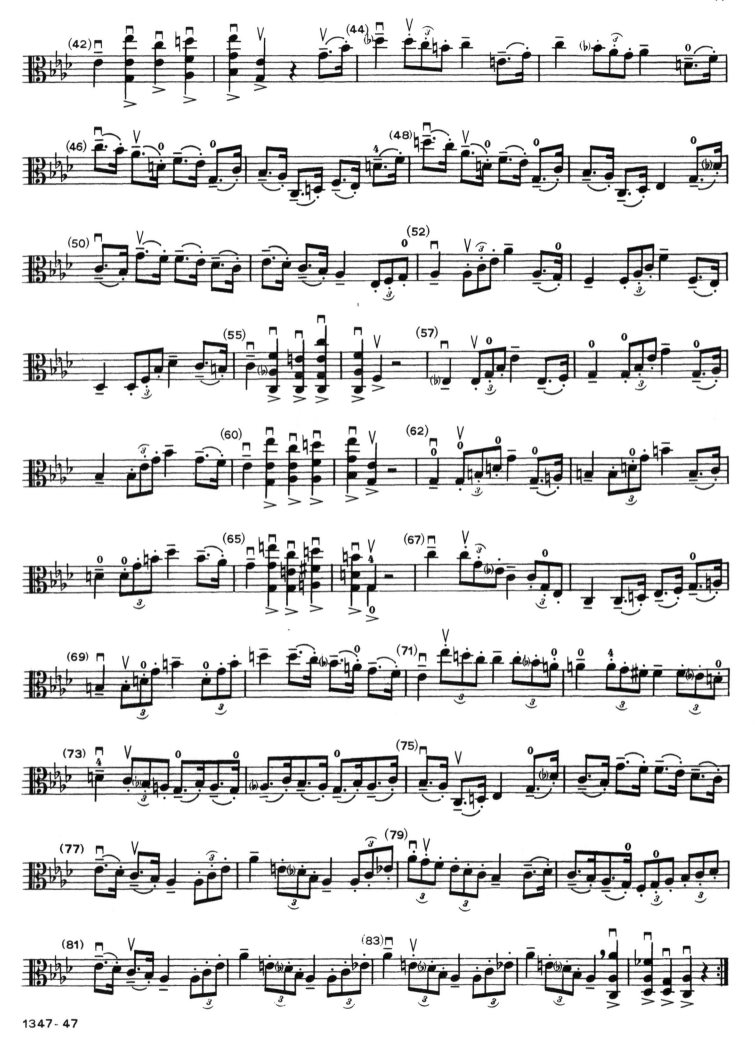

Etude - Finale

WOHLFAHRT

Practice slowly at first, Play as many notes as possible in each trill. Listen to both tones of every octave to be sure they are in tune with each other. Do not proceed from one interval to the next until the intonation is correct.